This book belongs to

_____

Jackie Robinson

By Mary Nhin

Illustrated By
Yuliia Zolotova

This book is dedicated to my children - Mikey, Kobe, and Jojo.

Copyright © 2022 by Grow Grit Press LLC. All rights reserved. No part of this book may be reproduced in any form without permission in writing from the publisher. Please send bulk order requests to growgritpress@gmail.com Printed and bound in the USA. MiniMovers.tv
Paperback ISBN: 978-1-63731-643-6 Hardcover ISBN: 978-1-63731-645-0

In college, I was the school's first athlete to win varsity letters in four sports: baseball, basketball, football, and track.

JOHN MUIR HIGH SCHOOL

I soon left to serve in the military, but when I came back I had a dream to play professional baseball.

The problem was that, during that time, there were 400 players in Major League Baseball, and all 400 players were white.

Then in 1947, everything changed. The Dodgers wanted me to play for them and I agreed. I became the first black Major League Baseball player.

My whole journey was tough, especially in the beginning, when my teammates didn't want to play with me because of the color of my skin.

During games, my opponents and fans would call me mean names and yell unkind things at me.

Pitchers tried to hit me in the head with fastballs.

Runners tried to injure me.

I received many death threats saying me and my family would be hurt if I continued to play.

It hurt me a lot to hear negative things said about me. I just wanted to play the game, but I knew I had to summon the strength to withstand it.

I believed with my whole heart that I was paving the way for future generations. I had to remain mentally tough not just for me and my family, but for others who depended on me.

My hard work, patience, and grit paid off. I soon made friends and fans, on and off the field. I slowly overcame my critics through grace and grit.

One time, an opposing player was saying mean things to me and my teammate stood up for me.

You can hate a man for many reasons. Color is not one of them.

Soon, all kinds of people were cheering for me. The whole country began to see that all people, despite the color of their skin, should be included in the sport of baseball, and all areas of life.

It helped people understand how important diversity and inclusion is. I think sports can be a lot like life. You face challenges in sports, but what matters most is how you respond to those challenges. In life, it's the same thing.

Many people say I changed the sport of baseball and the world.

I say baseball changed me. Sports has taught me about grit, grace, and hard work. These skills helped me to win, in baseball and in life.

Timeline

1947 – Jackie plays for the Dodgers

1947 – Jackie is awarded the inaugural Major League Baseball Rookie of the Year Award

1949 – Jackie wins the National League Most Valuable Player Award

1955 – Jackie and his team win the World Series

1962 – Jackie is inducted to Hall of Fame

minimovers.tv

 @marynhin   @officialninjalifehacks
#minimoversandshakers

 Ninja Life Hacks

 Mary Nhin   Ninja Life Hacks

 @officialninjalifehacks

www.ingramcontent.com/pod-product-compliance
Lightning Source LLC
Chambersburg PA
CBHW041523070526

44585CB00002B/55